Sacred Geometry

Designs to Cut out for Crystal Grids or other uses.

www.sweetharmonypress.com

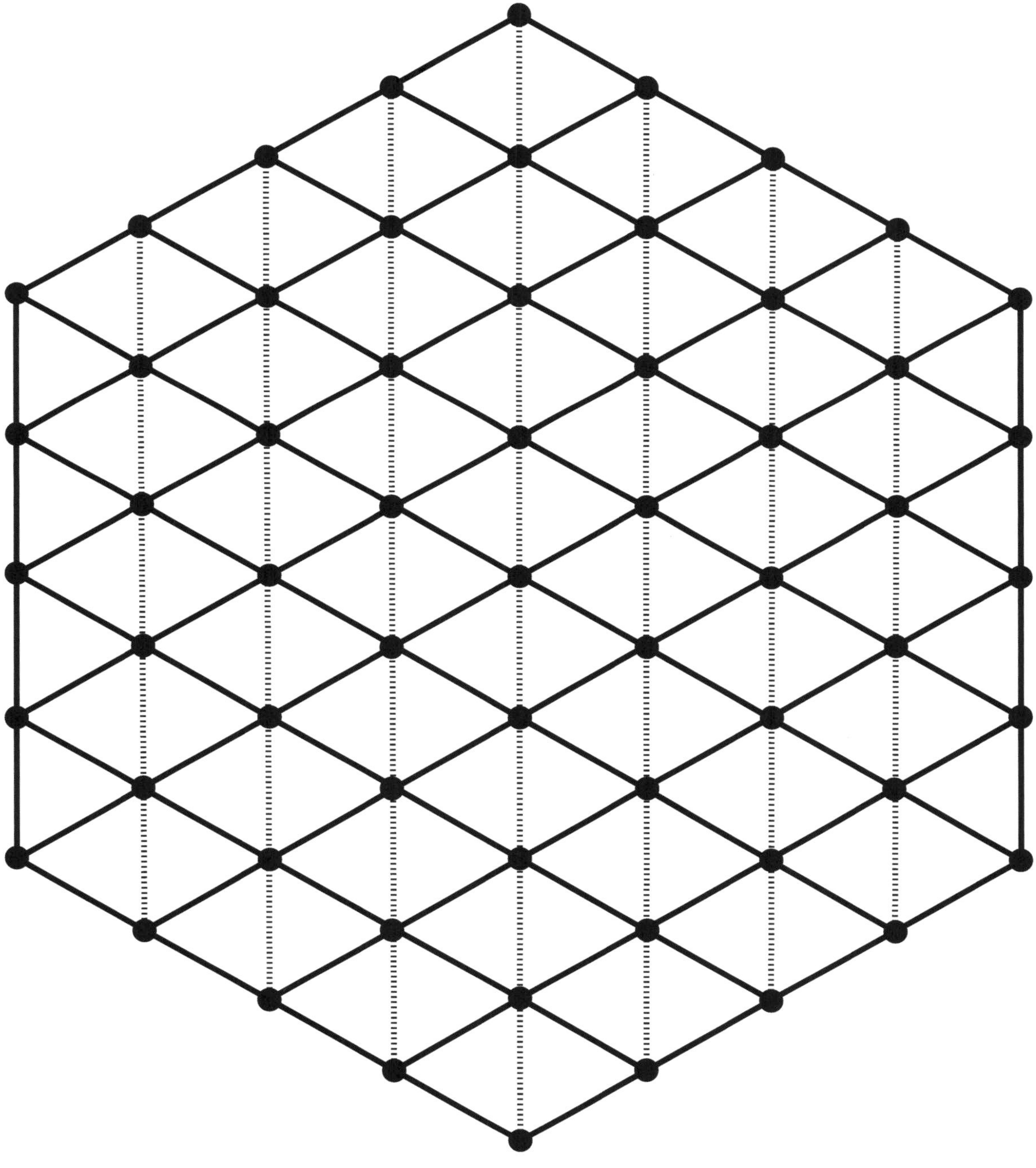

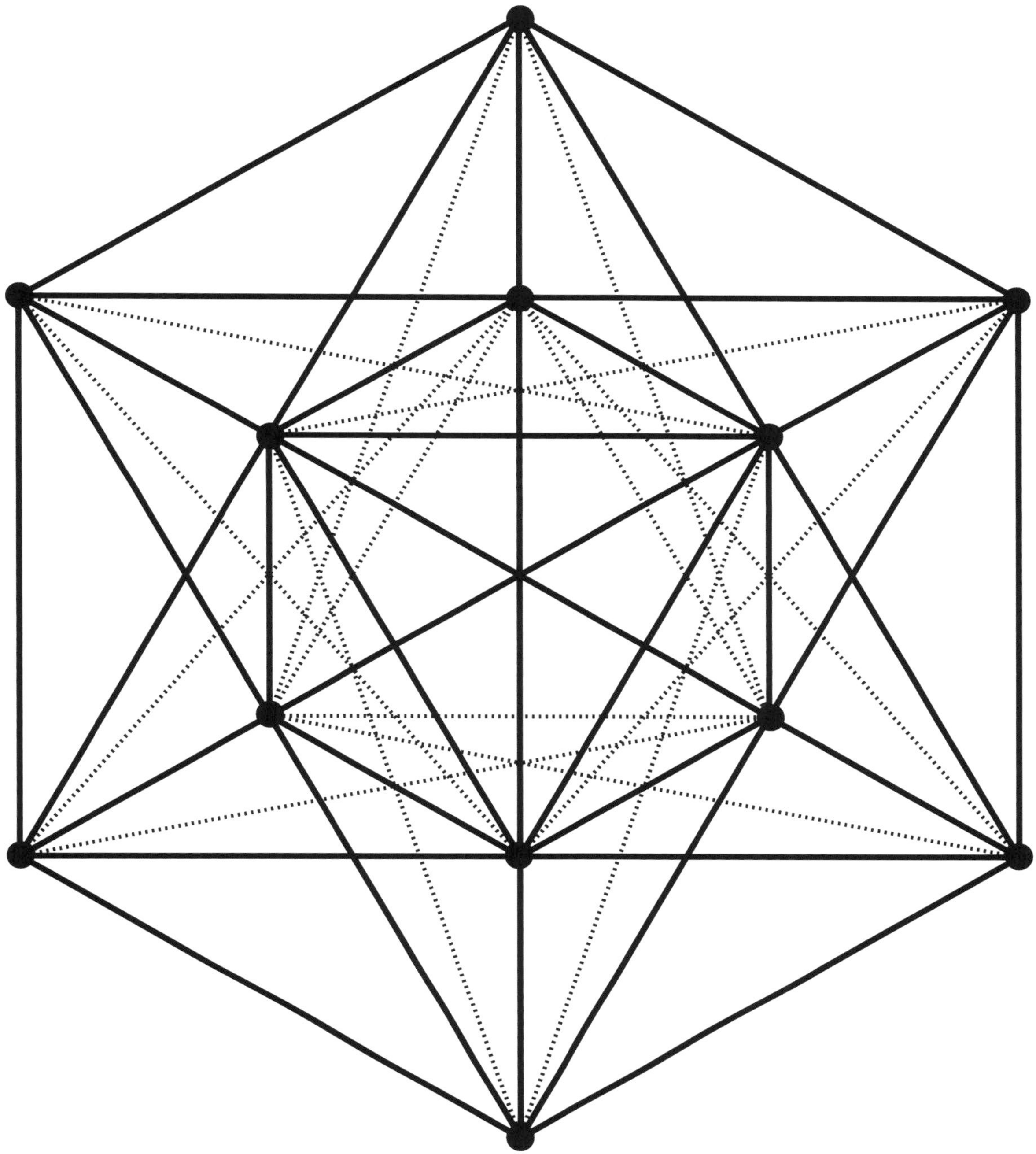

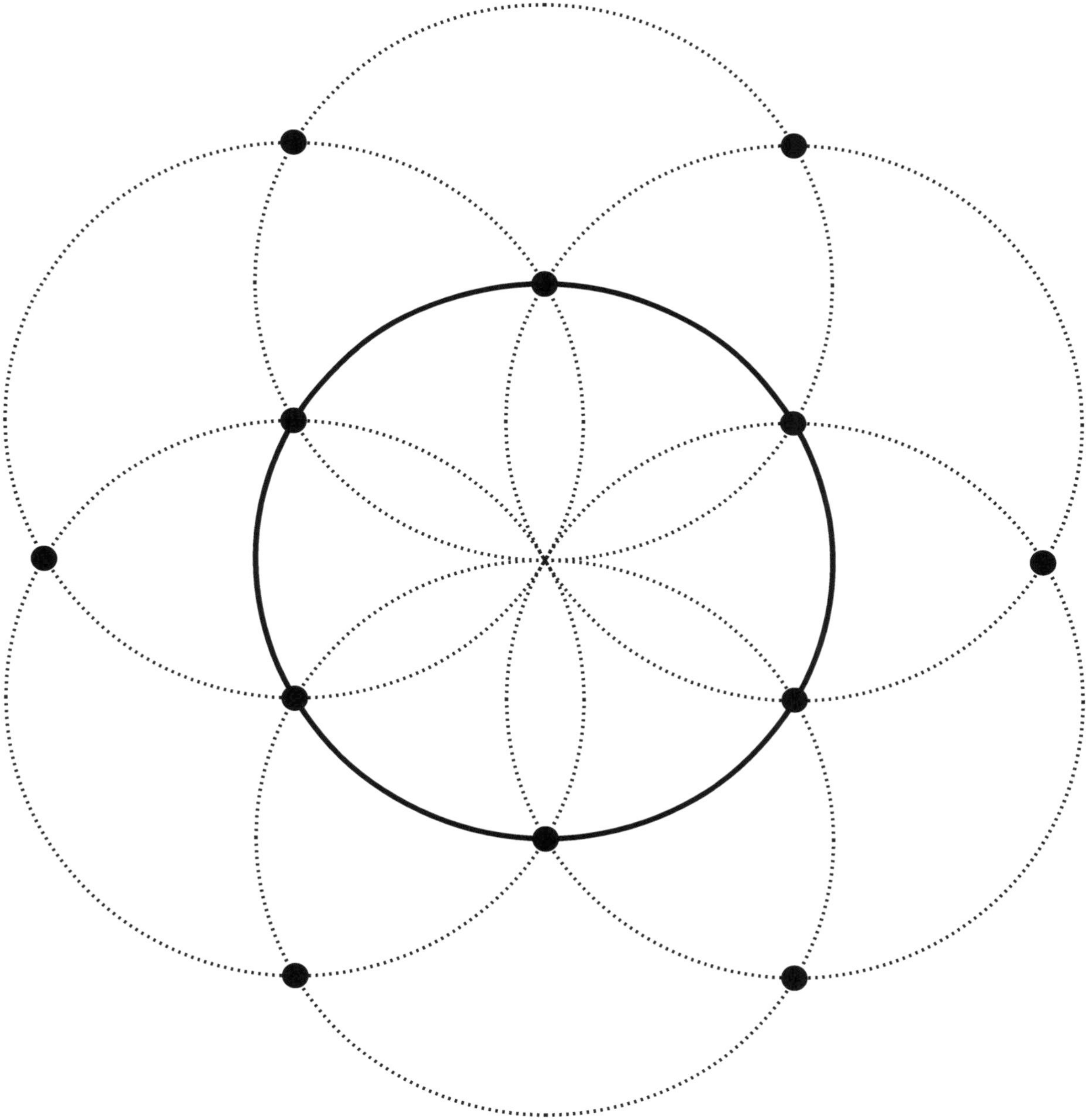

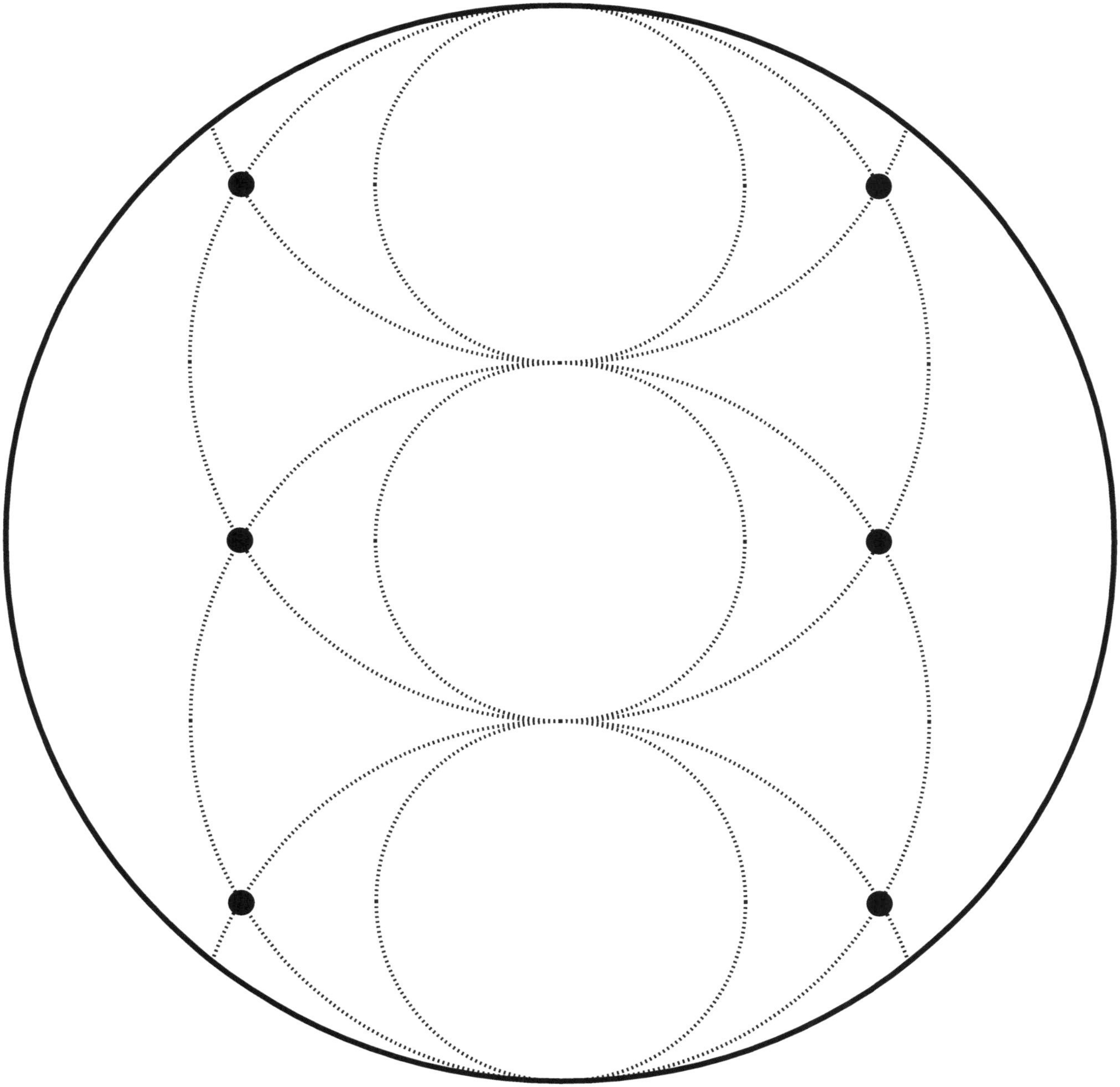

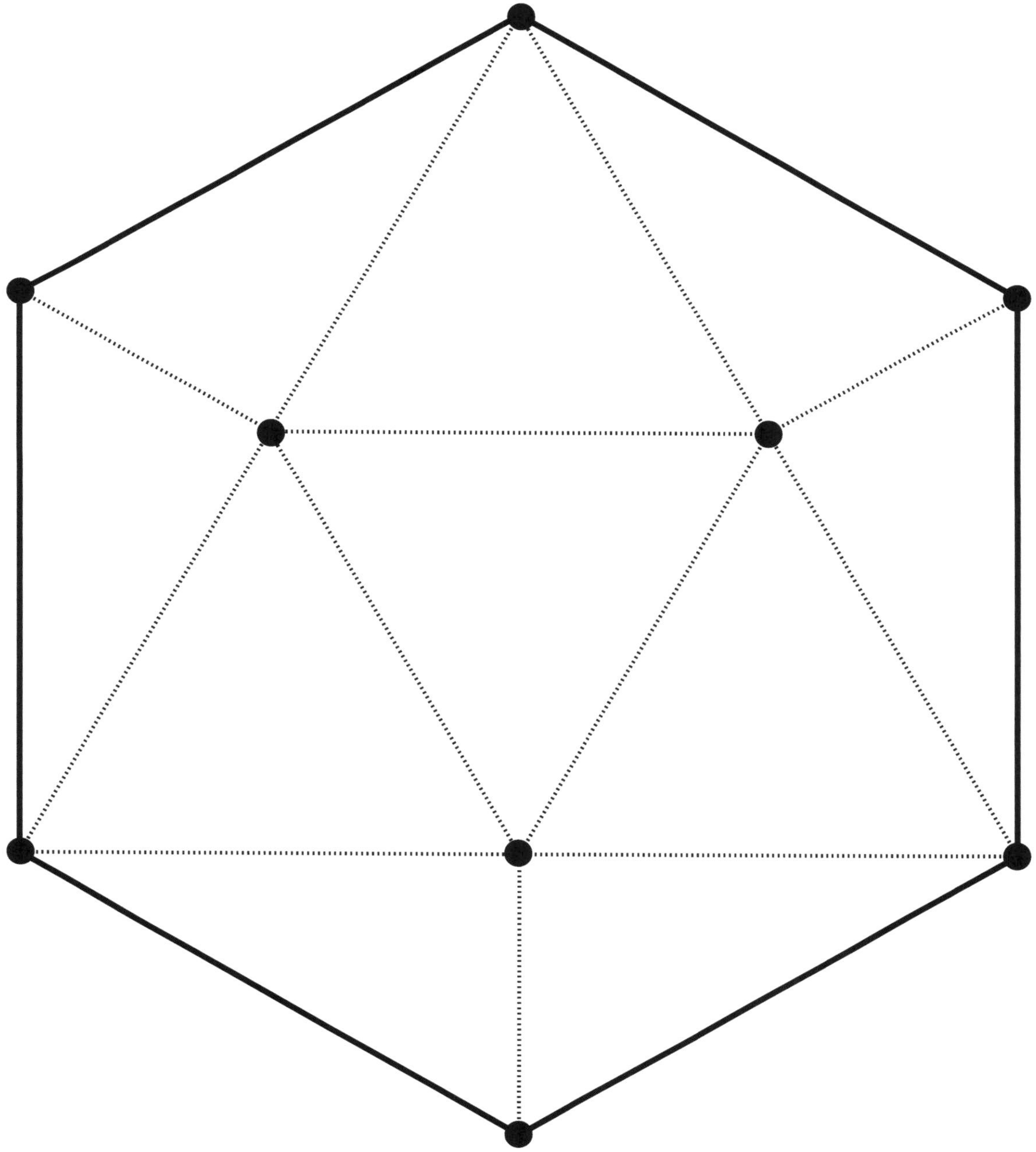

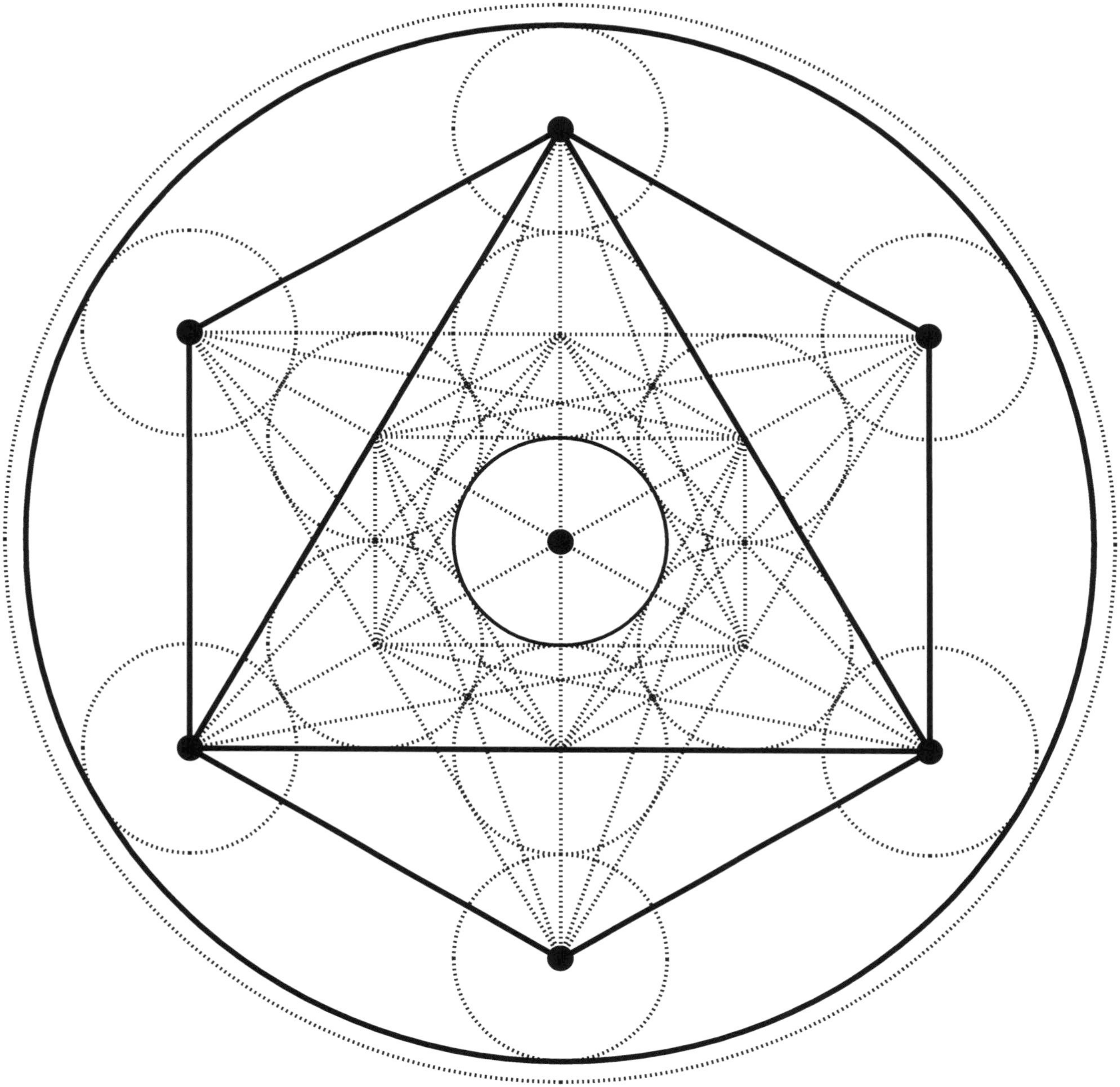

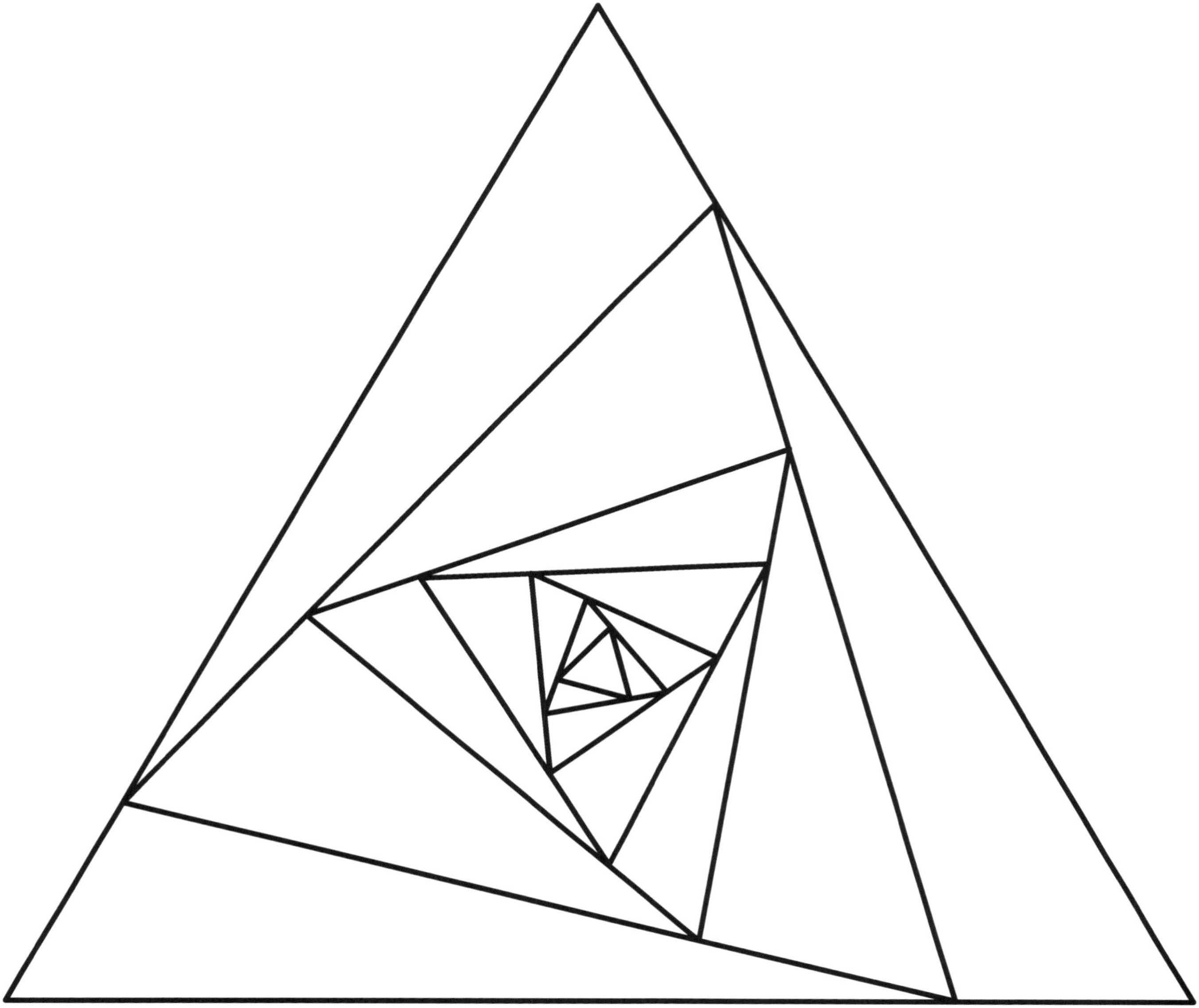

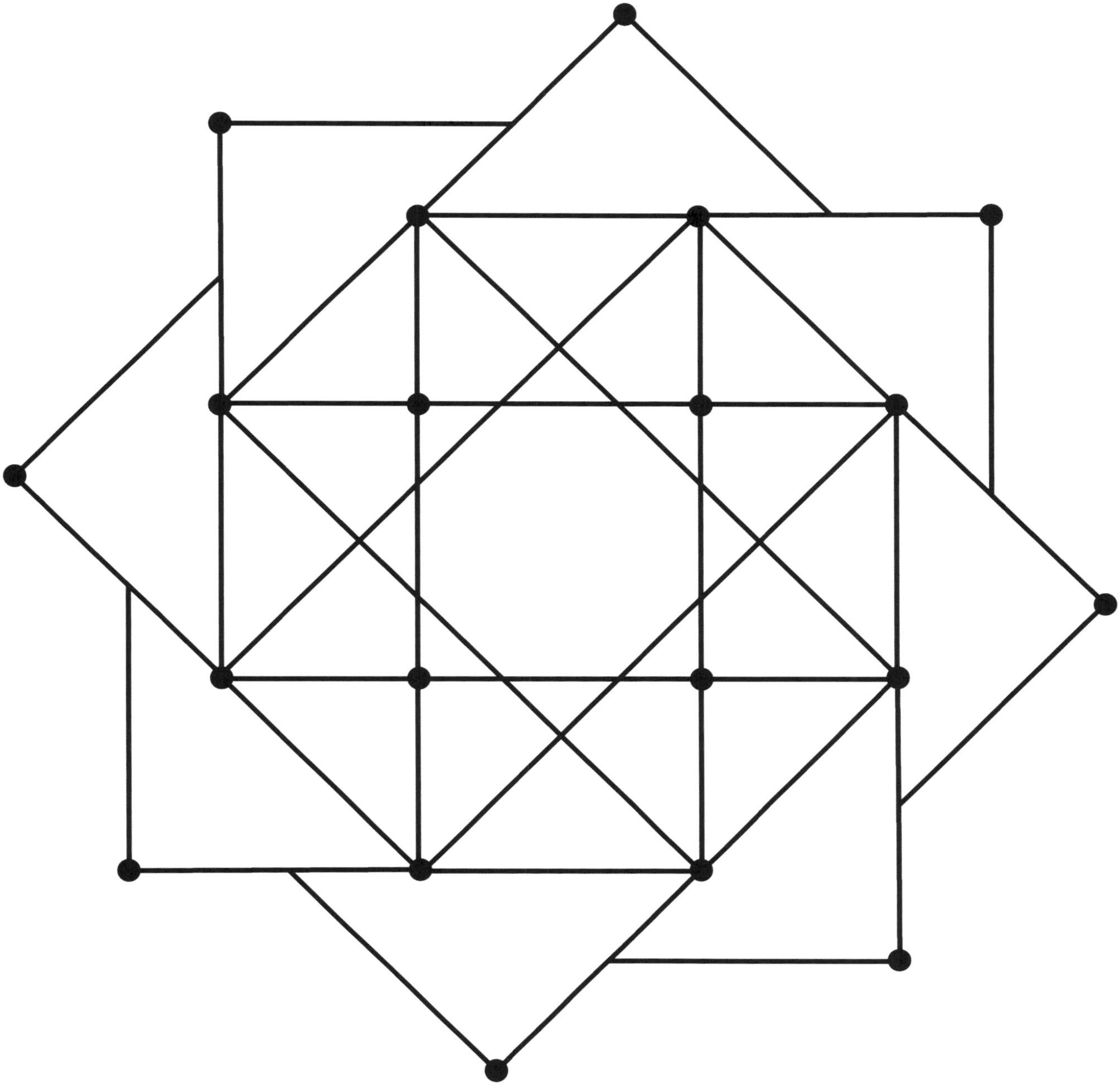

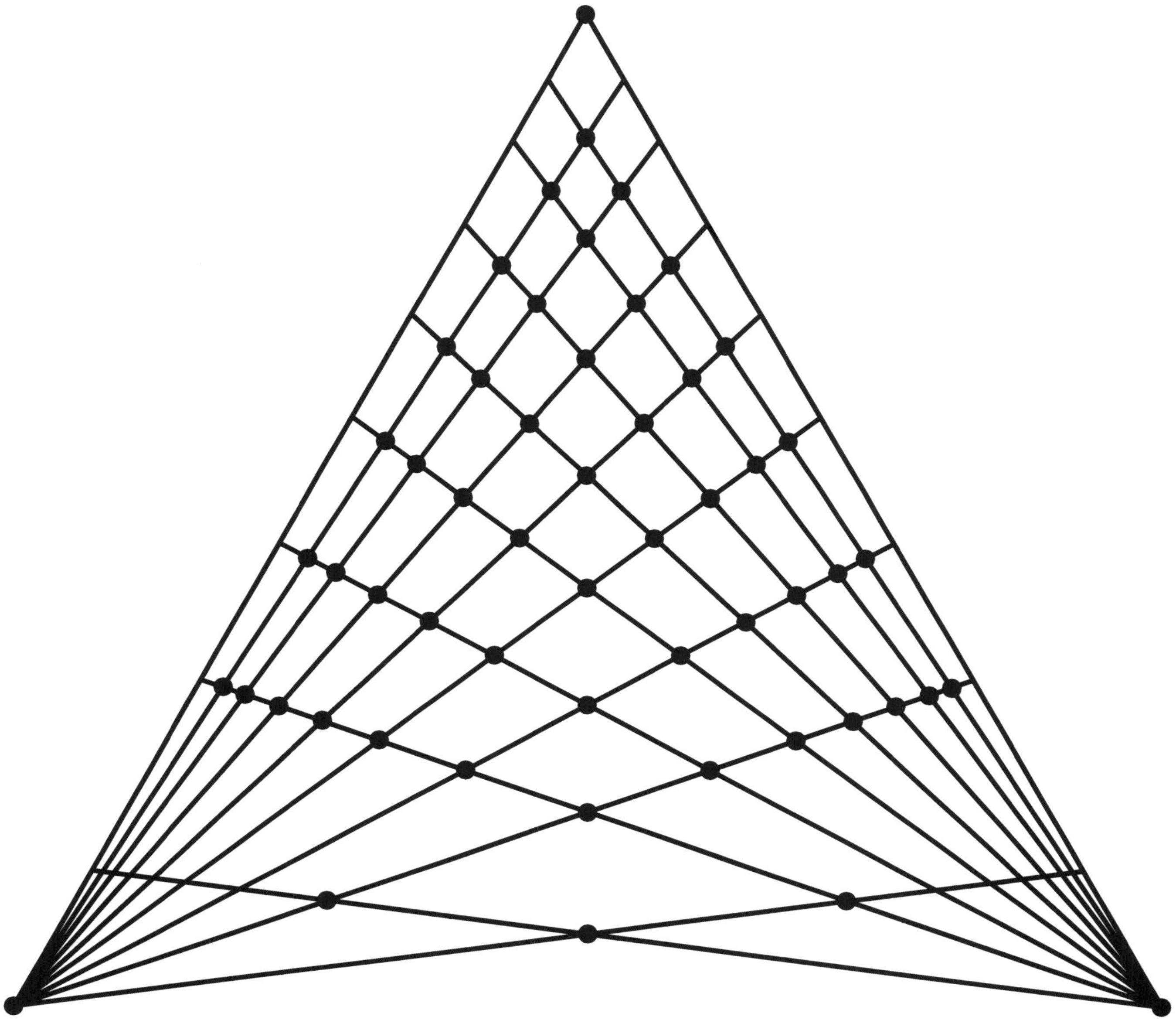

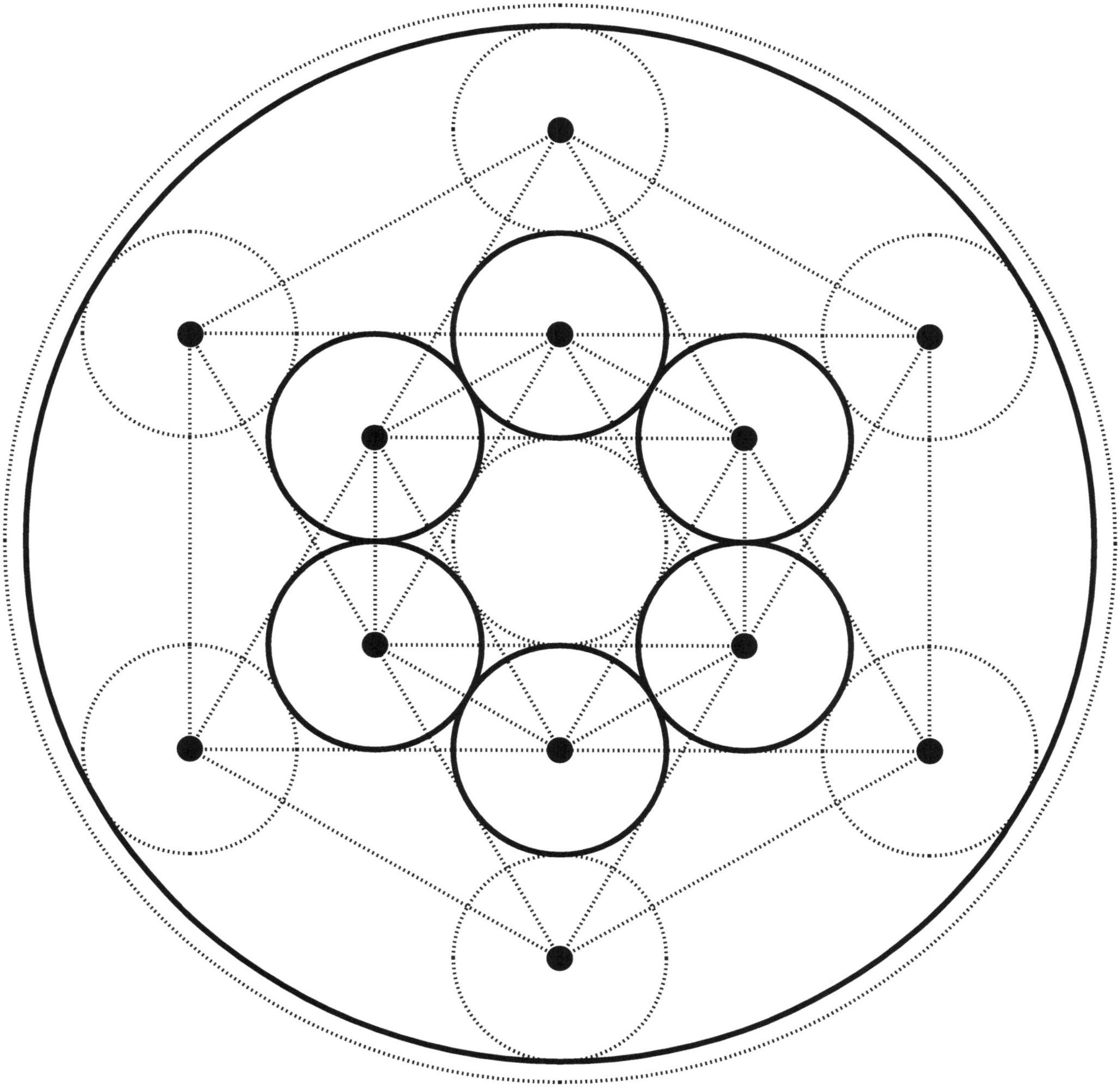

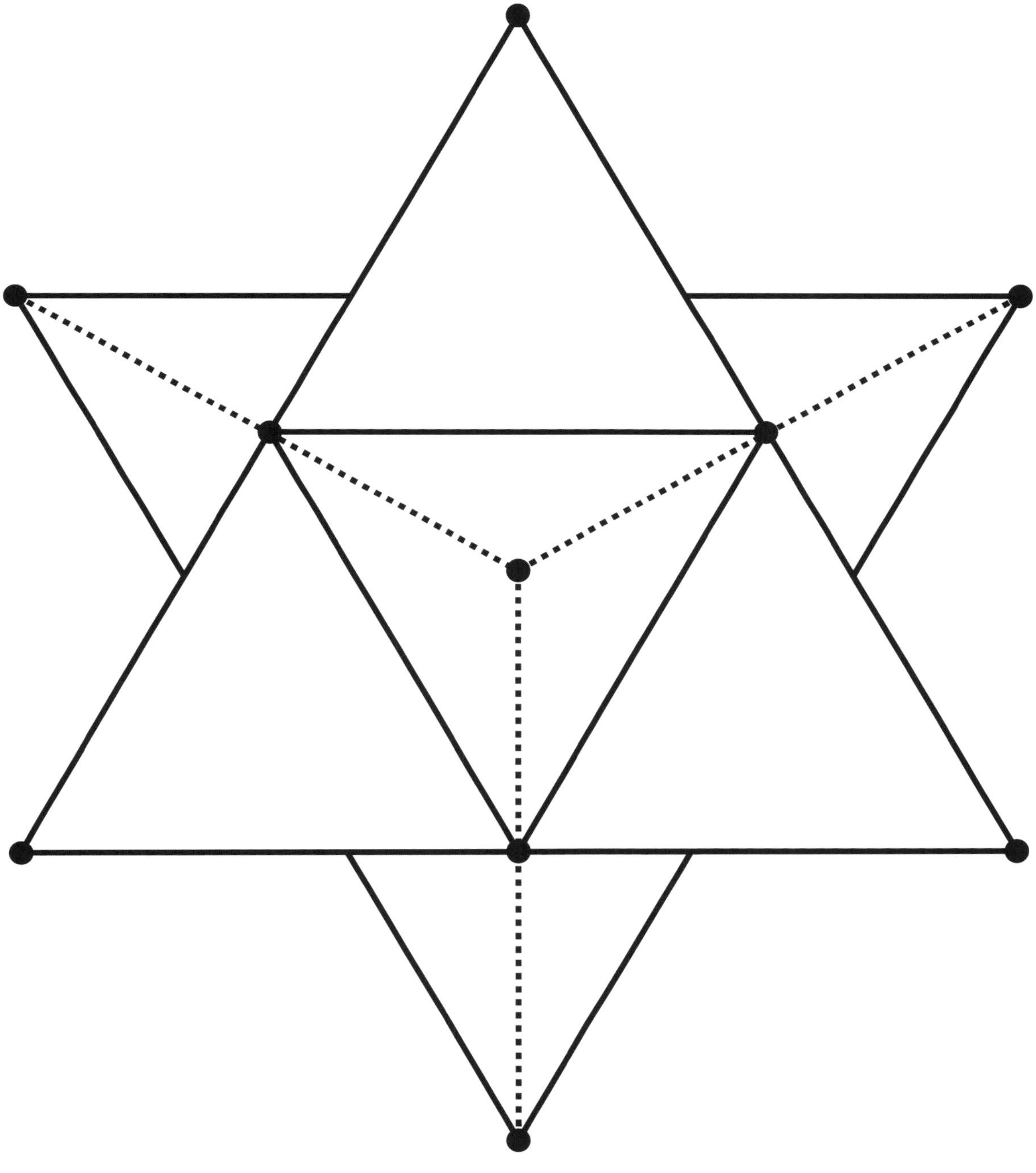

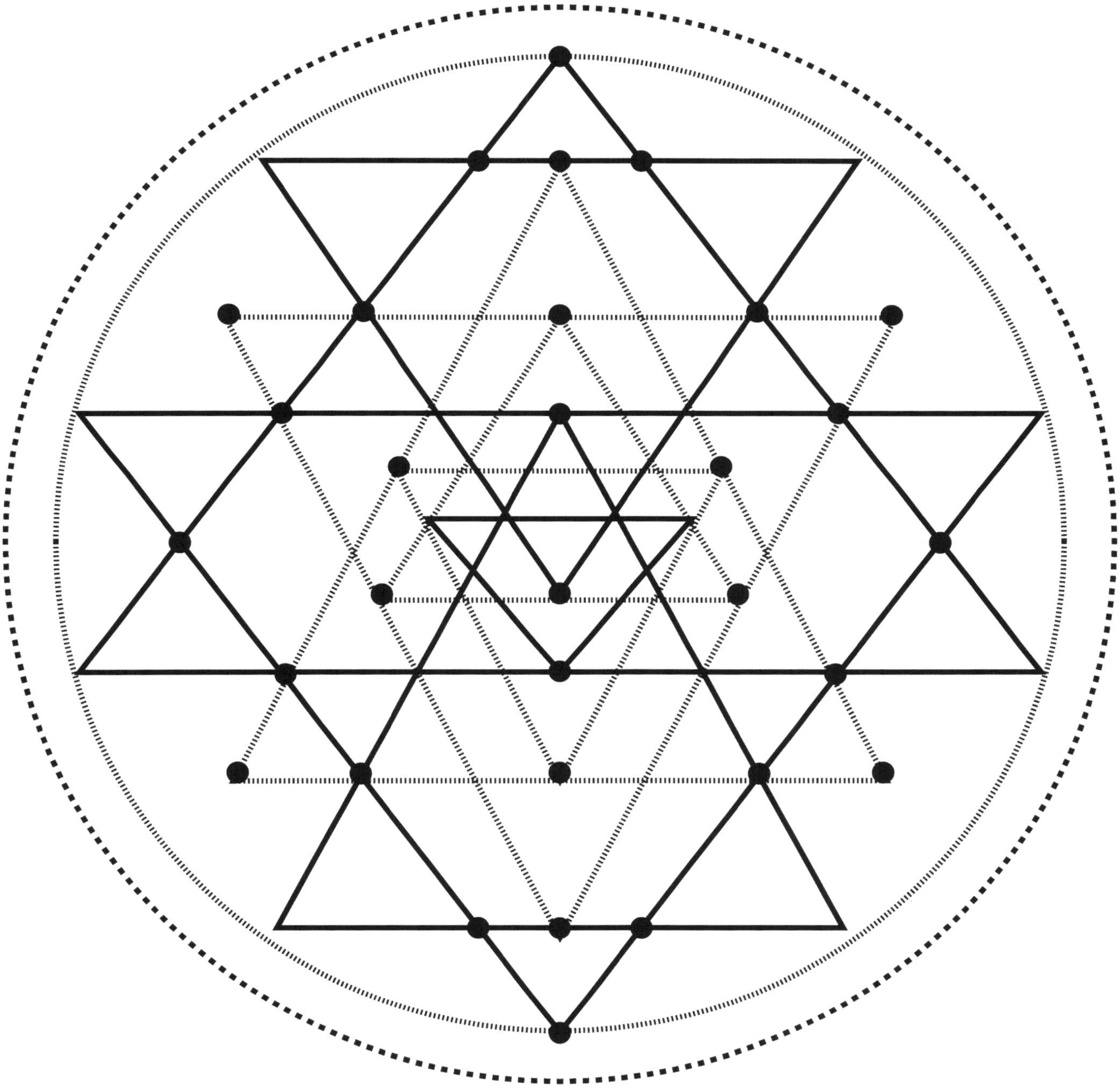

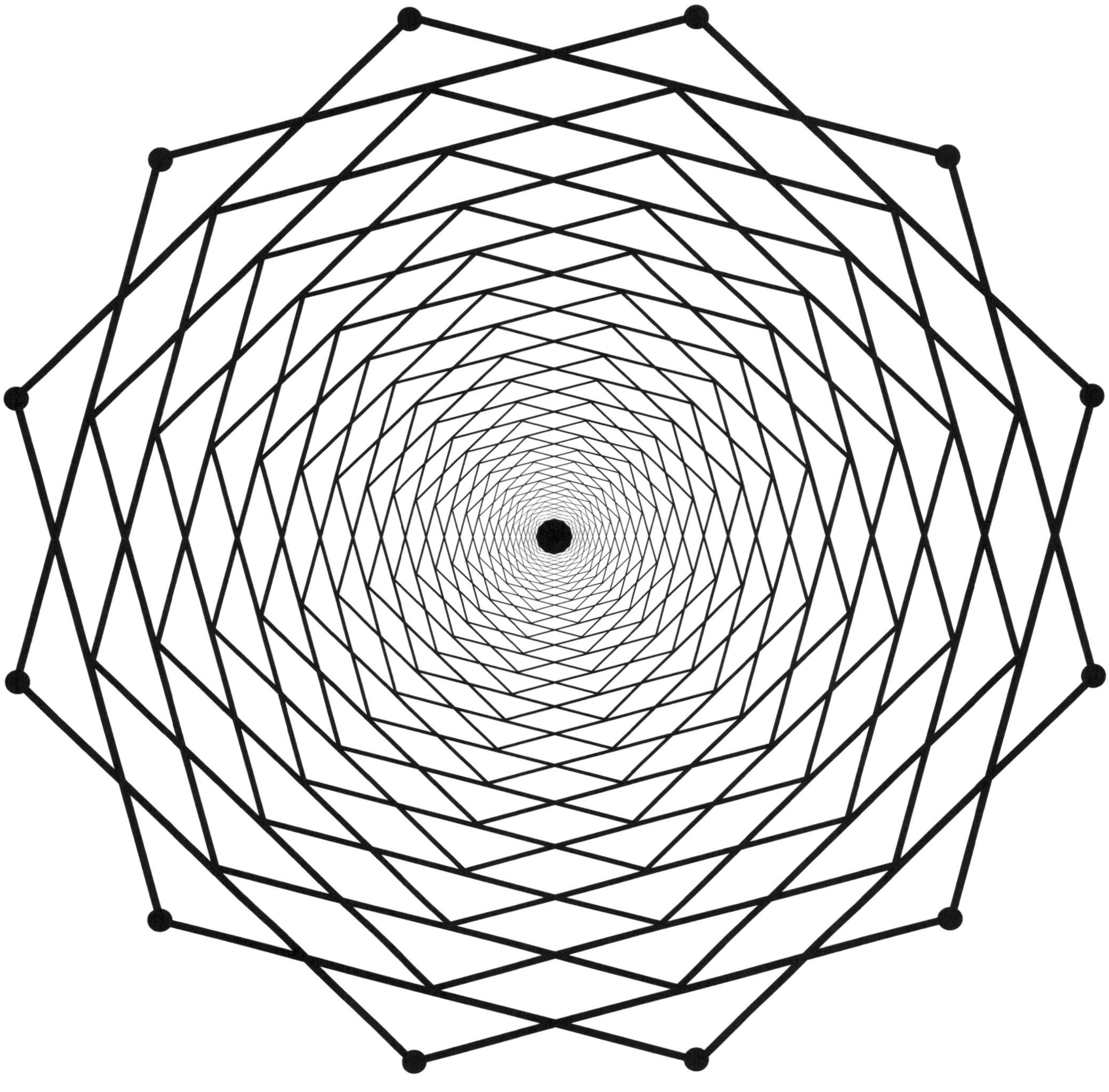

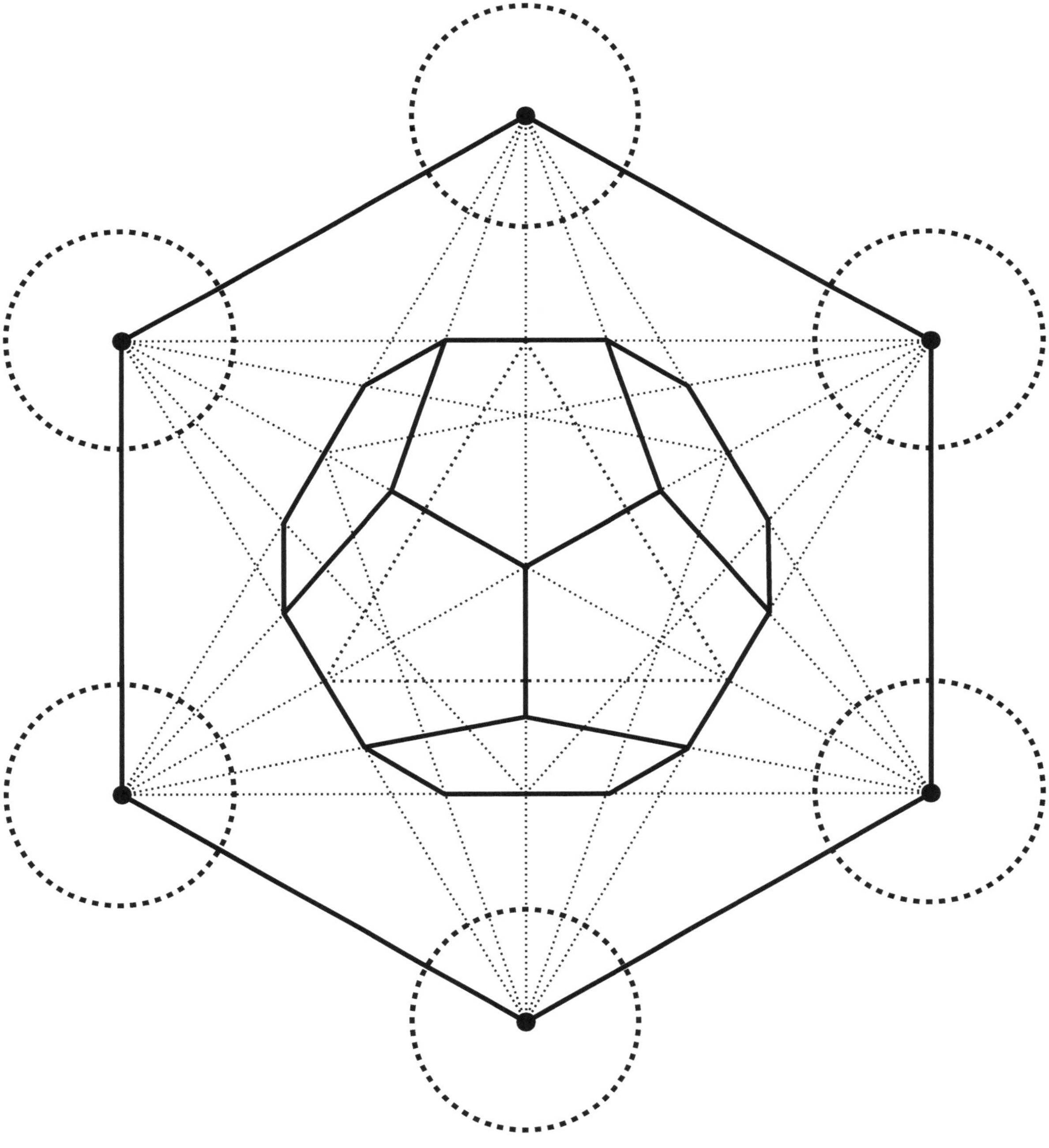

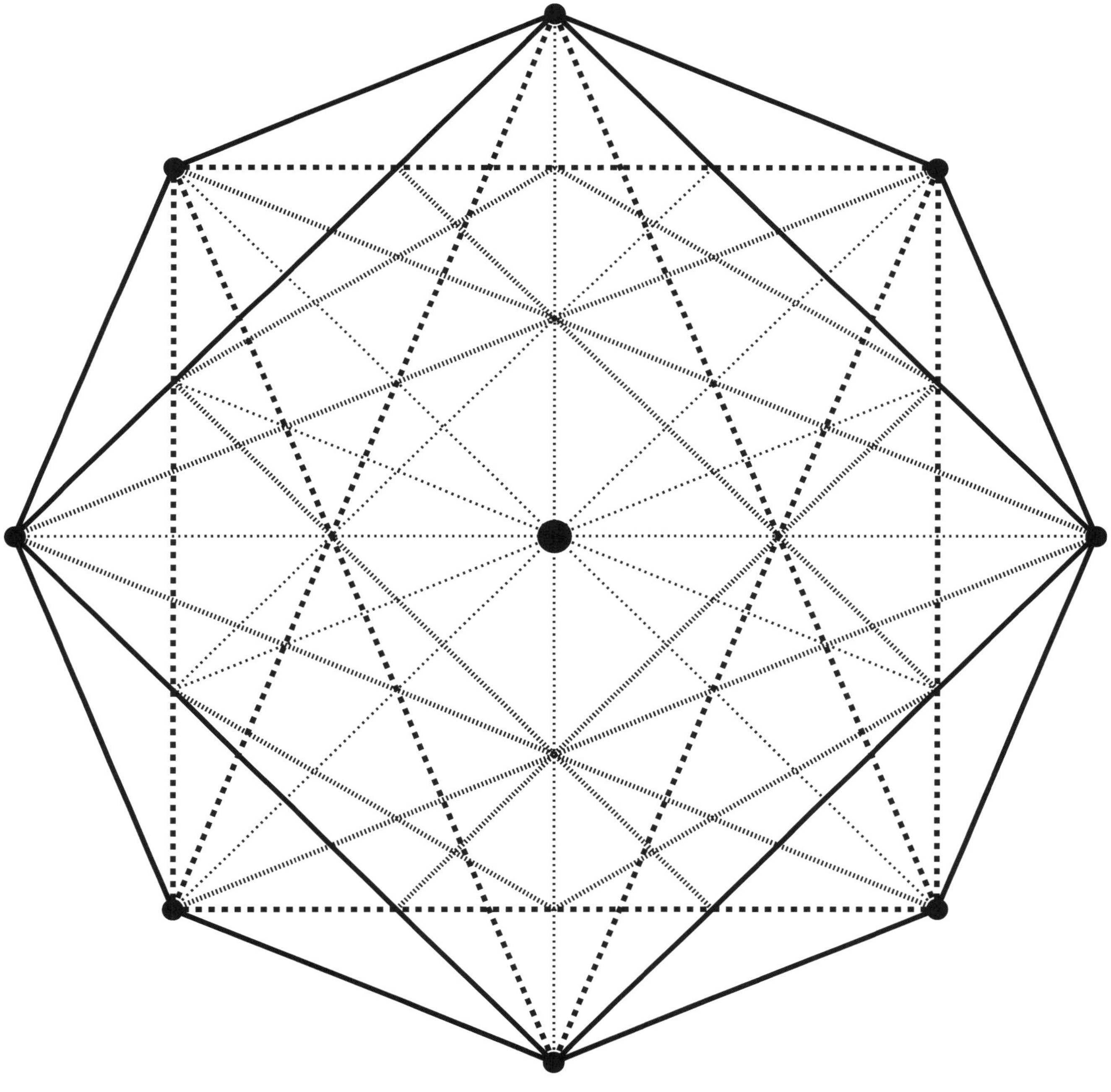

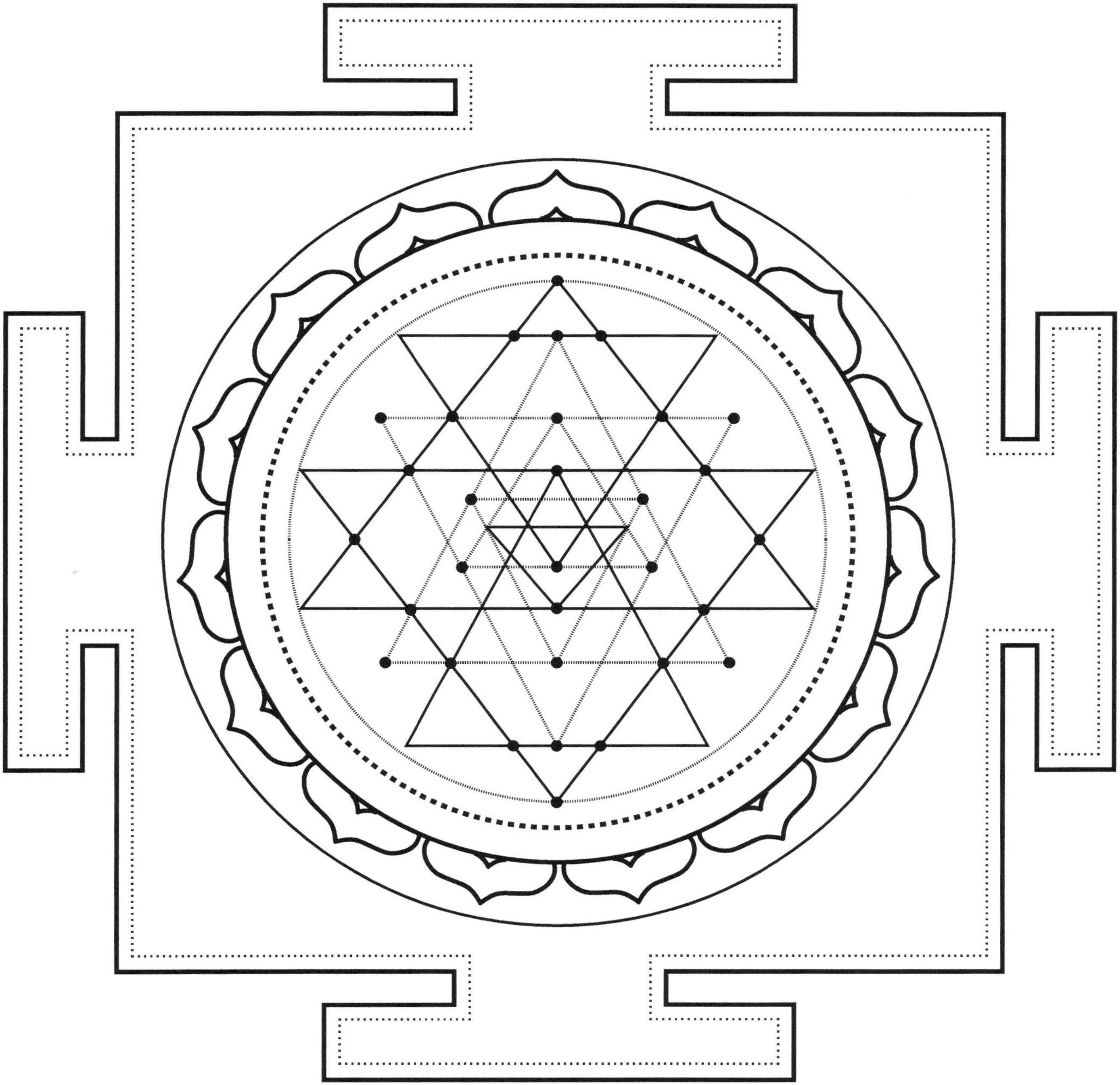

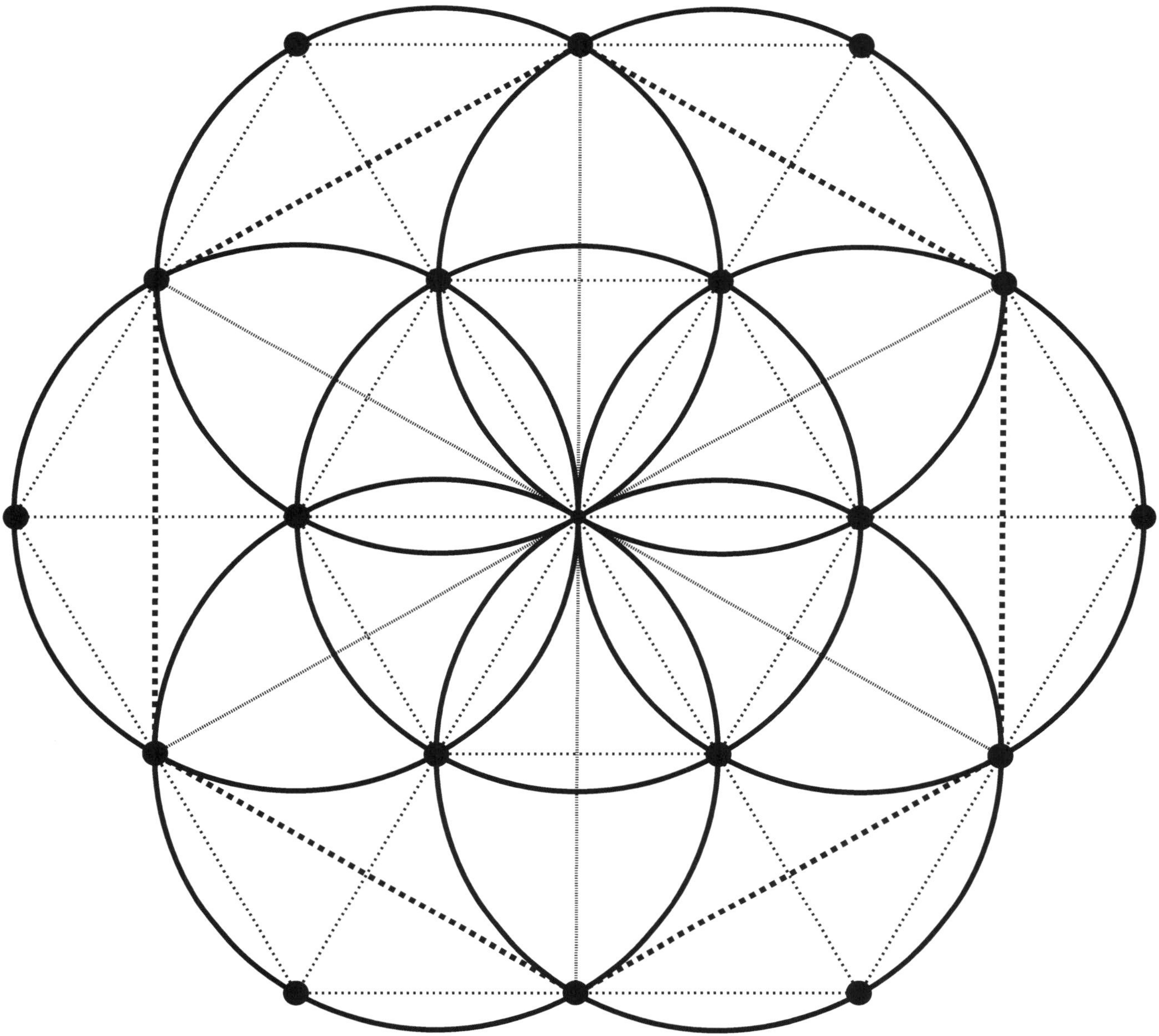

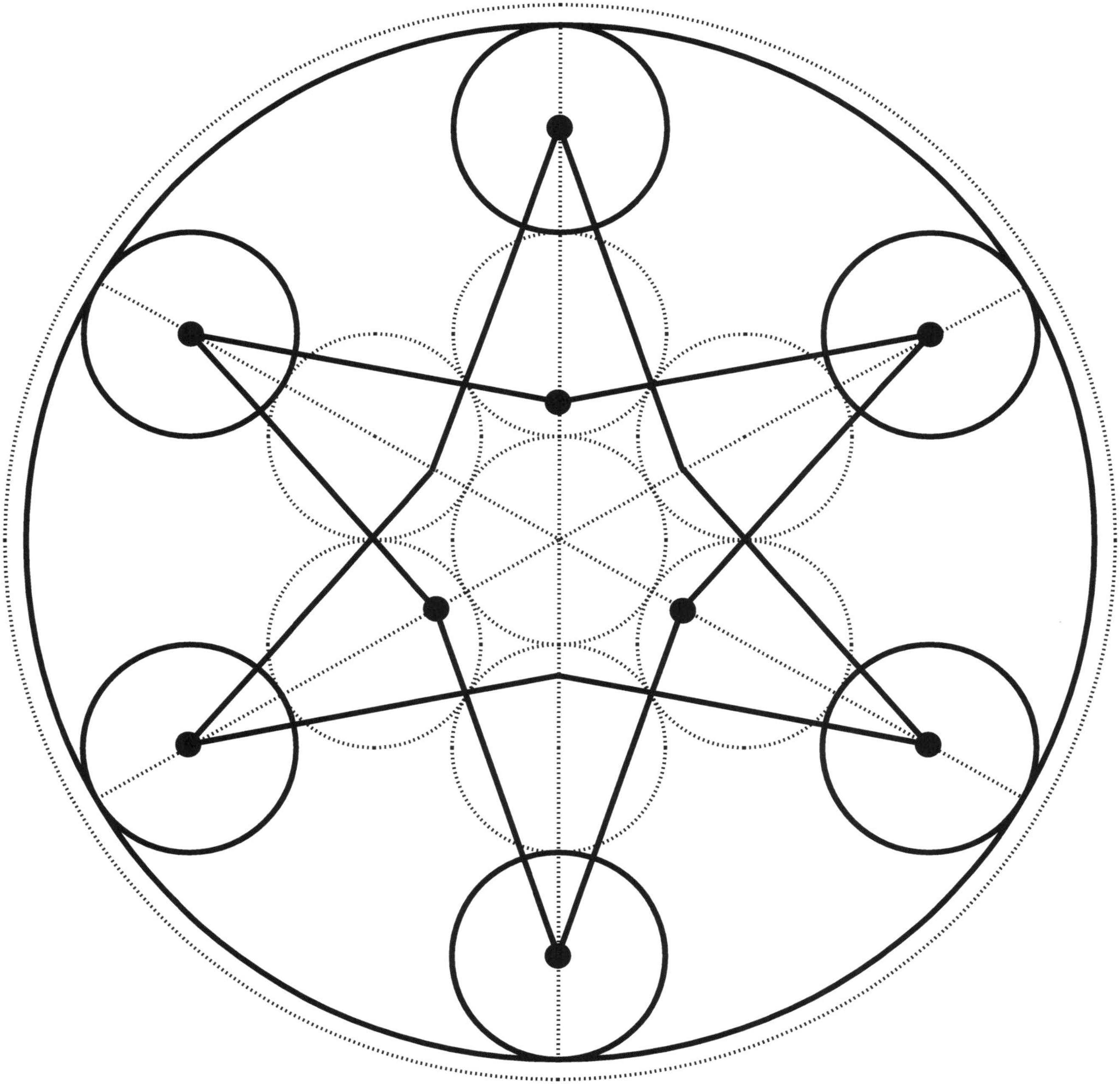

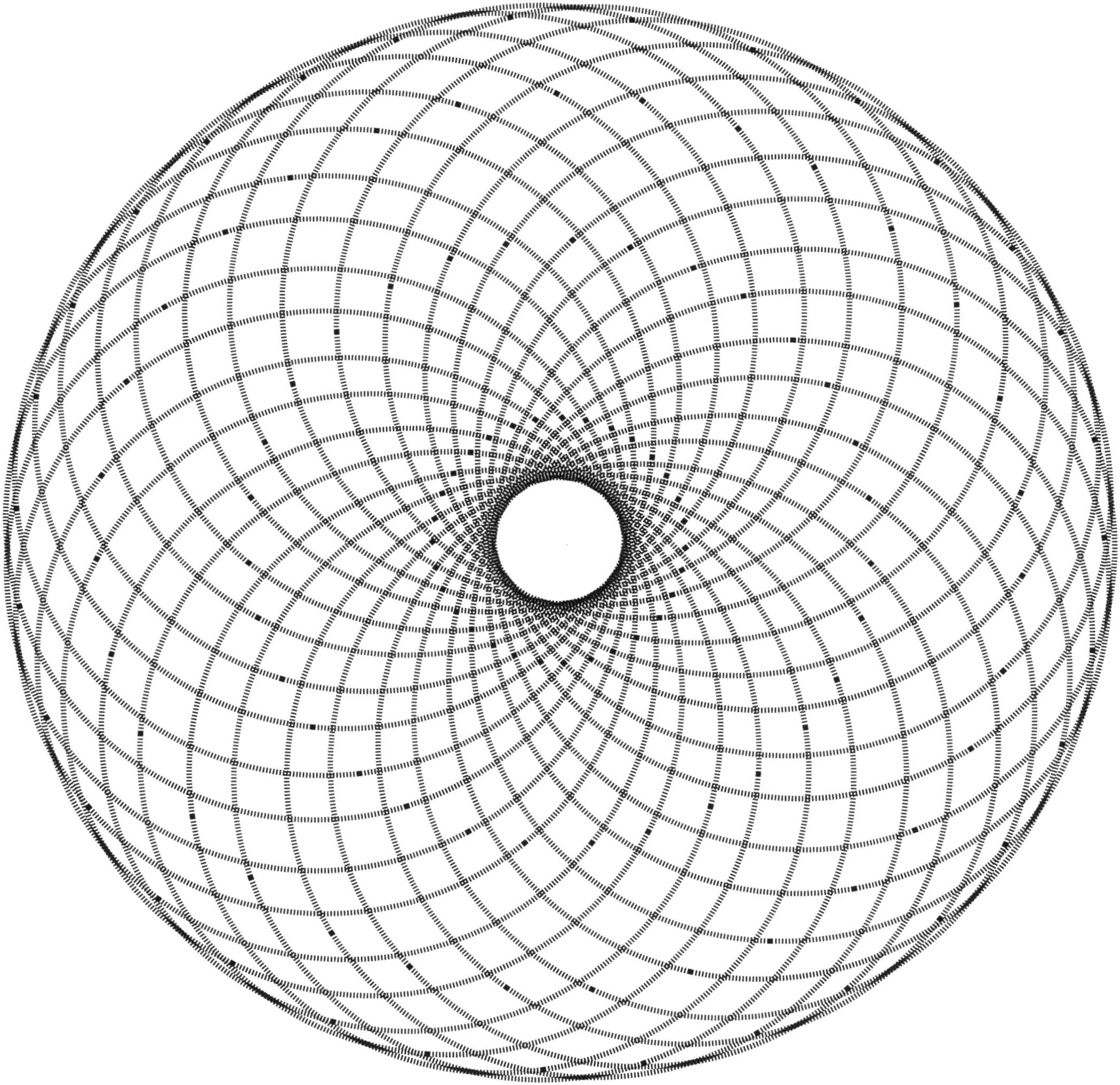

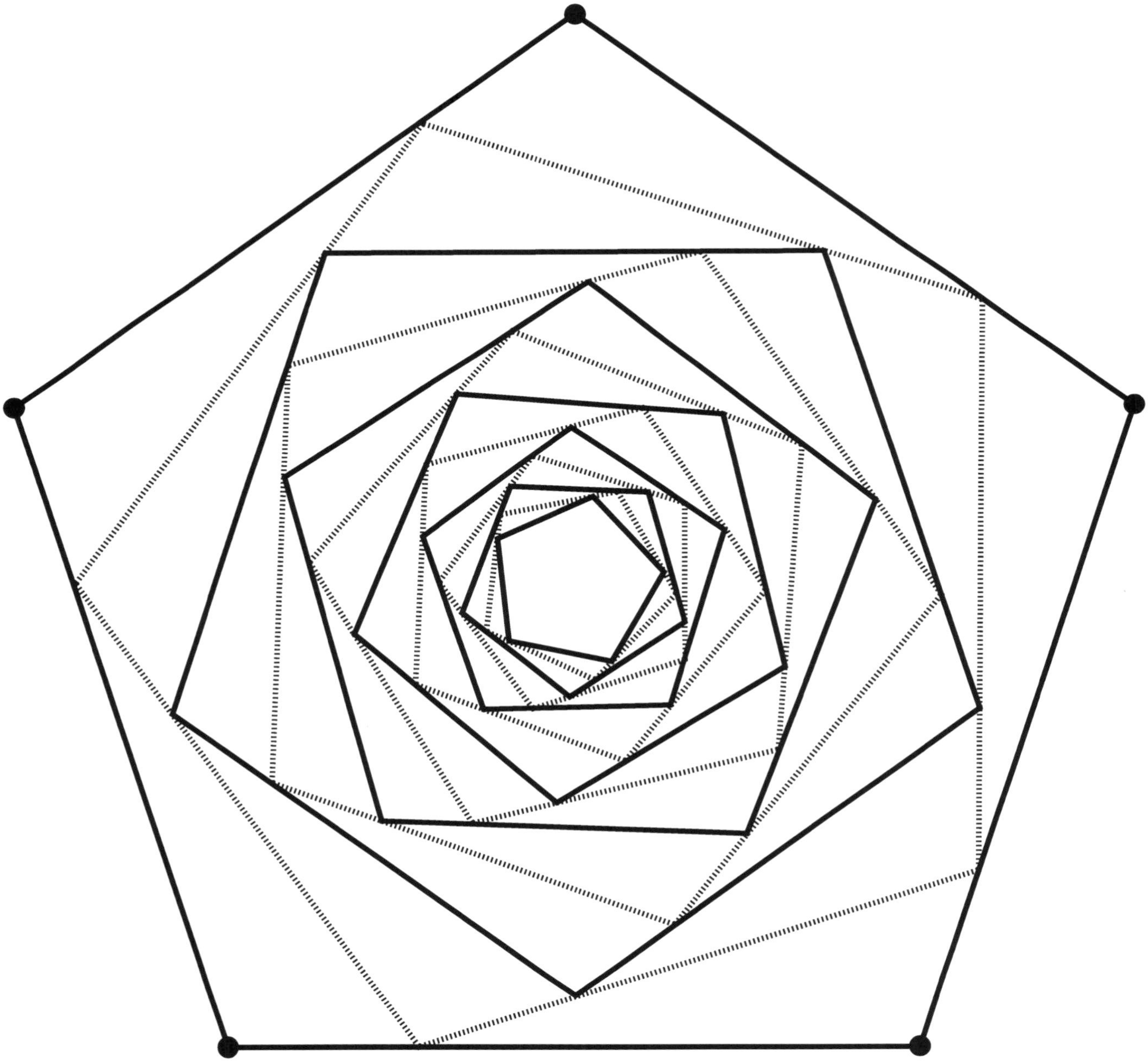

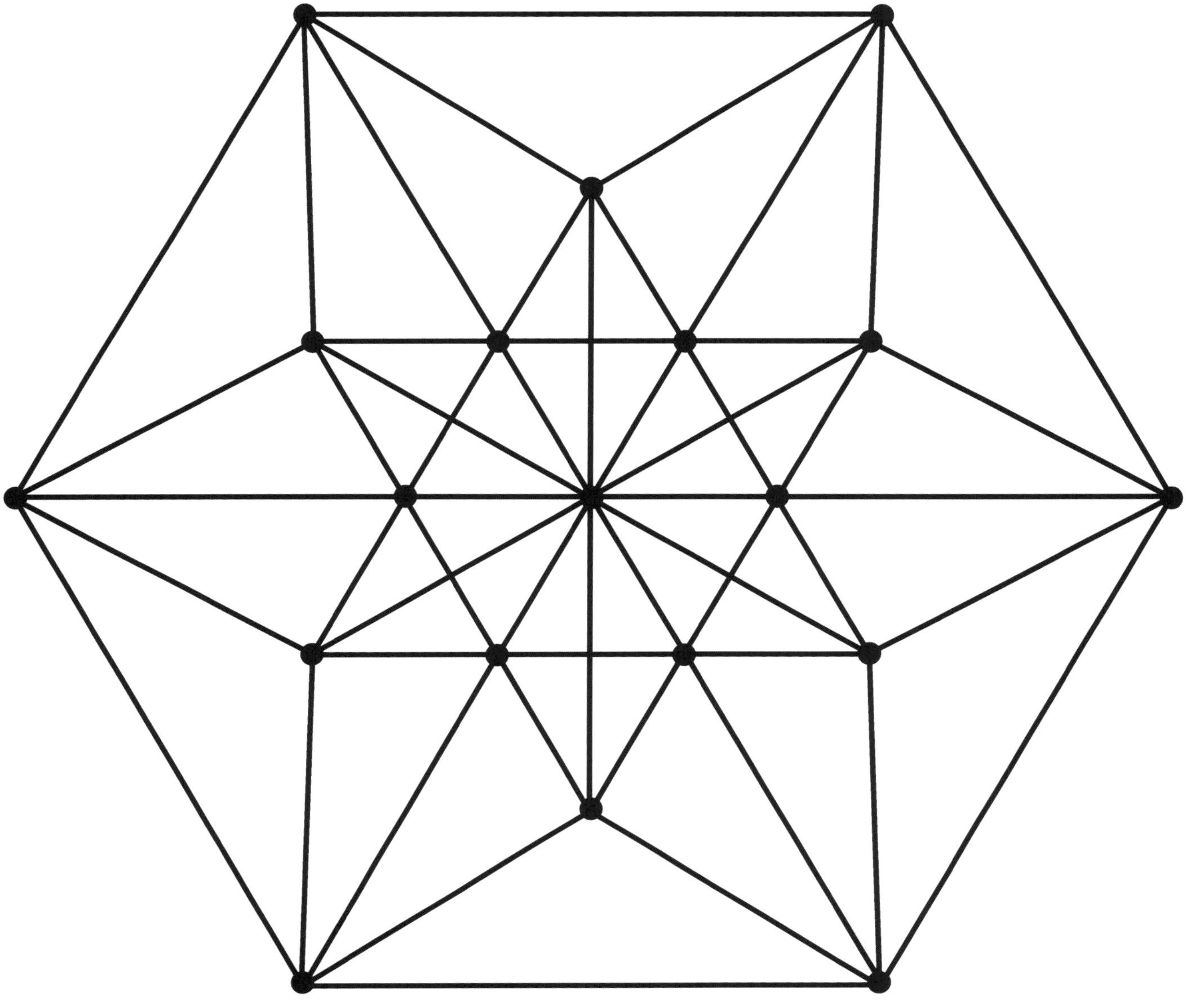

Manufactured by Amazon.ca
Bolton, ON

10330615R00028